Calligraphy is one of the most accessible of all the crafts because the tools and materials required are simple and relatively easy to get hold of. It is also one of the most satisfying. Not only can calligraphy be used functionally for writing names on cards, bookmarks and invitations, but for those who love words, calligraphy can create beautiful artworks which will give pleasure and delight. This booklet shows you how to write the four basic calligraphic scripts, each of which has a project which takes you from producing a professional looking card using one letter to creating a calligraphy artwork.

La calligraphie compte parmi les moyens d'expression artistiques les plus accessibles car les outils et le matériel nécessaires sont simples et relativement faciles à obtenir. Ce fascicule vous montre comment écrire les quatre scripts de calligraphie de base, illustrés par des projets qui vous guident de la réalisation d'une carte décorée d'une lettre, digne d'un professionnel, à la création d'une œuvre calligraphique.

De todas las manualidades, la caligrafía es una de las más asequibles ya que los útiles y los materiales necesarios son sencillos y fáciles de adquirir. Este folleto muestra los cuatro estilos caligráficos básicos; cada uno de ellos presenta un proyecto con orientaciones que le permitirán crear desde una tarjeta profesional utilizando una sola letra hasta una obra de arte caligráfica.

1

Getting Started

A broad-edged calligraphy pen makes the characteristic thicks and thins of calligraphy letters, and is kept at the same angle to the horizontal for the different writing styles. You can use a calligraphy fountain pen, felt tip or calligraphy dip pen. Right-handers should use straight cut nibs, and left-handers, left oblique.

I Left-oblique nibs for left-handers; straight cut nibs for right-handers.

Choose paper with a smooth surface (HP or hot pressed). Ordinary photocopying paper is a good start. Calligraphy layout paper is perfect for practice as it is thin and you can see guidelines drawn on another sheet of paper beneath. This guideline sheet can then be used again and again; simply put another piece of layout paper over the top.

Letters in calligraphy are written with separate strokes, and the pen lifted between them. The stroke direction and order is shown by the red arrow and the grey number on the letter-forms.

II A board which slopes at about 45° will mean that your back is straight, and your pen horizontal when you write. Ink will then only come out of your pen when you put pressure on it, and so should not flood. Try to ensure that your feet are flat and firmly on the floor for stability. You could instead rest a sheet of wood in your lap and prop it on a table edge.

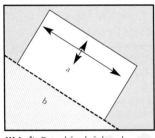 

a. Slide your work paper behind the guard sheet. Keep your hand at the same comfortable level; the paper moves, as shown by the arrows.

b. Tape a piece of paper as a guard-sheet across your board to protect your work.

III Left: Board for left-handers;   **Right**: and for right-handers.
Tape sheets of paper as a pad to your board to make a comfortable writing surface.

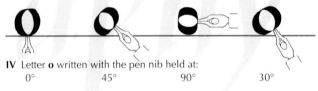

IV Letter **o** written with the pen nib held at:
0°   45°   90°   30°

The height of the letters relates to the width of the nib being used. Turn the nib so that it is horizontal to determine the heights of letters, and make a series of little steps which just touch and do not overlap.

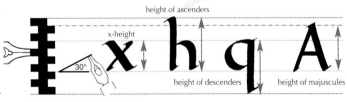

III Letters which start with a curved stroke to the left

These letters should be round and fat. The second stroke making the bowl of the letter e should not be too low, otherwise the letter looks unbalanced.

Alternative forms of **a** and **g**

IV Diagonal letters

*The first diagonal stroke is quite shallow. This makes the letter wide. Apart from the letter **w** these letters should be about the width of the letter **o**.*

*Turn the nib to an angle of 10° for the diagonal stroke

V Letters which do not fit these family groups

*Choose the simpler forms of the letters **a** and **g** if you find them easier. Keep the top stroke of the letter **f**, and the last stroke of the letter **g** flat and open so they do not look like fishhooks! The middle part of the letter **s**, and the looped part of the letter **g** should be smooth curves; practise making this stroke sinuous and avoid sharp bends or angles.*

VI Numerals, ampersand, and punctuation marks

abcdefghijklmnopqrstuvwxyz

Prise en main

*U*n stylo de calligraphie à pointe large permet de former les pleins et les déliés caractéristiques des lettres calligraphiées, et doit être maintenu au même angle par rapport à l'horizontale pour les différents styles d'écriture. Vous pouvez utiliser un stylo plume, un feutre ou un porte-plume de calligraphie. Les droitiers devraient utiliser des plumes taillées droites, et les gauchers, des plumes obliques à gauche.

Choisissez un papier avec une surface lisse (pressé à chaud). Le papier ordinaire pour photocopie convient bien pour commencer. Le papier translucide de calligraphie est parfait pour s'entraîner car il est mince et vous pouvez voir les lignes de la portée dessinées sur une autre feuille de papier en dessous. Cette feuille directrice peut être utilisée maintes et maintes fois, il suffit de placer une nouvelle feuille d'écriture par-dessus.

En calligraphie, les lettres sont formées en traits séparés, en soulevant sa plume entre chaque trait. Le sens et l'ordre des traits sont indiqués par la flèche rouge et le chiffre gris sur les dessins des lettres.

I La hauteur des lettres se rapporte à la largeur de bec de la plume utilisée.

II Un plan incliné à environ 45° vous permettra d'avoir le dos droit et votre plume horizontale lorsque vous écrivez. Posez vos pieds à plat et fermement sur le sol pour assurer la stabilité. Vous pouvez également placer une planche de bois sur vos genoux en la soutenant sur le bord d'une table.

III À l'aide d'un ruban adhésif, fixez des feuilles de papier sous forme de bloc à votre planche pour créer une surface d'écriture confortable.

Gauche: pose d'un support pour gauchers; **droite**: pour droitiers.

IV Lettre *o* écrite avec la plume tenue à: 0°, 45°, 90°, 30°.

La hauteur des lettres se rapporte à la largeur de bec de la plume utilisée. Pivotez la plume à l'horizontale pour déterminer la hauteur des lettres et faites une série de petits paliers qui se touchent à peine et ne se chevauchent pas.

Cómo empezar

*U*n bolígrafo caligráfico ancho dibujará los característicos trazos gruesos y finos de las letras de caligrafía, manteniendo el bolígrafo al mismo ángulo horizontal para los diferentes estilos de escritura. También pueden utilizarse estilográficas, rotuladores o plumas caligráficas. Se recomienda que las personas diestras utilicen plumines de corte recto mientras que las personas zurdas deberían utilizar plumines de corte oblicuo a izquierdas. Seleccione un papel con una lisura uniforme y suave (hp o calandrado). El papel normal para hacer fotocopias es una opción excelente para empezar. El papel de calco caligráfico es perfecto para practicar ya que es fino y permite ver las líneas de guía dibujadas en la hoja de papel debajo. De esta forma, la hoja de guía puede utilizarse una y otra vez, colocando encima otra hoja de papel de calco.

En caligrafía las letras se dibujan con trazos separados y el bolígrafo se levanta entre ellos. La dirección y el orden del trazo están indicados por la flecha roja y los números grises en las formas de las letras.

I La altura de las letras viene dada por el ancho del plumín utilizado.

II Un tablero inclinado 45° aproximadamente hará que la espalda de escritor esté recta y el bolígrafo horizontal cuando escriba. Procure asegurar que los pies estén planos y bien apoyados sobre el suelo para mayor estabilidad. También puede apoyar un tablero de madera en el regazo y apoyarlo en el borde de la mesa.

III Utilice cinta adhesiva para pegar hojas de papel sobre el tablero y hacer una superficie de escritura cómoda.

Izquierda: Colocando un tablero para personas zurdas; **Derecha**: y para personas diestras.

IV Letra *o* escrita sujetando el bolígrafo a: 0°, 45°, 90°, 30°.

La altura de las letras viene dada por el ancho del plumín utilizado. Gire el plumín de forma que esté horizontal para determinar la altura de las letras y haga una serie de pasos pequeños para justo tocar pero sin solapar.

Using calligraphy metal nibs

Utilisation des plumes
Utilizar plumines caligráficos

The crispest letter-forms are made with pen nibs which have the sharpest tips. Quills, specially cut flight feathers from swans, geese and other birds, were used in mediæval manuscripts, and much of the lettering in these books is spine-tinglingly fine.

Nowadays we mainly use metal nibs held in calligraphy dip pens, as they are more convenient and the nibs last longer; it is possible to achieve wonderfully crisp letters with these also.

Most calligraphy dip pens need to be assembled. Push the nib into the pen holder so that it is firm and does not wobble. After you have finished writing, wash and dry the nib and reservoir separately.

I Ensure that the reservoir touches the nib and is about 2mm (0·08 inch) from the tip of the nib so that it feeds in the ink.

II To avoid a blob of ink when you start writing feed the ink into the side or under the nib using an old paint brush, rather than dipping in ink.

III Get your pen to write by making narrow strokes first. When the ink is flowing you can then make thicker strokes.

Ce sont les plumes les mieux taillées qui produisent les dessins de lettres les plus nets. Les pennes de cygne, d'oie et d'autres oiseaux étaient utilisées pour les manuscrits du Moyen-Âge, et les écritures dans ces livres sont d'une finesse saisissante.

De nos jours nous utilisons principalement des plumes métalliques insérées dans des porte-plume de calligraphie car elles sont plus pratiques et durent plus longtemps ; elles permettent tout autant de réaliser des écritures remarquablement nettes.

La plupart des porte-plume de calligraphie doivent être assemblés. Poussez la plume dans son support, elle doit être tenue fermement, sans osciller. Après avoir finir d'écrire, lavez et séchez la plume et le réservoir séparément.

I Veillez à ce que le réservoir touche la plume et qu'il se trouve à environ 2 mm de sa pointe pour l'alimenter en encre.

II Pour éviter de faire une tache d'encre lorsque vous commencez à écrire, déposez l'encre sur le côté ou sous la plume à l'aide d'un pinceau, plutôt que de tremper la plume dans l'encre.

III Amorcez votre porte-plume en faisant d'abord des traits étroits. Lorsque l'encre coule, vous pouvez faire des traits plus épais.

Utilizando plumines con las puntas más afiladas se logra formar las letras más nítidas. Las plumas, sobre todo las cortadas de las plumas remeras de los cisnes, gansos y otros pájaros, se utilizaban en los manuscritos medievales y muchas de las inscripciones en estos son soberbiamente finas.

Hoy en día utilizamos mayormente plumines de metal acoplados en estilográficas ya que son más prácticos y los plumines duran más; con estos útiles modernos también es posible lograr letras extremadamente nítidas.

La mayoría de las estilográficas necesitan montarse. Introduzca el plumín en el portaplumas firmemente para evitar que temblequee. Después de terminar de escribir, lave y seque el plumín y el depósito por separado.

I Compruebe que el depósito toque el plumín y que esté a aproximadamente 2mm de la punta del plumín para que alimente la tinta.

II Para evitar los borrones de tinta al empezar la escritura, alimente la tinta en el costado o debajo del plumín utilizando un pincel viejo, en lugar de sumergirlo en el tintero.

III Haga que el bolígrafo escriba haciendo trazos estrechos primero. Cuando la tinta empiece a fluir puede empezar a hacer trazos más gruesos.

Foundational or Round Hand Minuscules

These letters are based on those which were used in manuscripts written in England in the tenth century. This style is called the Foundational or Round Hand, or English Caroline Minuscule.

In this style, the letter **o** is round and fat, and all the letters take their form from this. Do not be mean and skimpy with your Round Hand letters – keep them circular. Hold your nib at an angle of 30° to the horizonal for these upright letters. See key on page 28.

The x-height for this alphabet is 4 nib widths. With a pencil and long ruler draw a series of parallel guidelines which are 4 nib widths apart on suitable smooth paper and start to practise the individual letters. However, rather than practising letters by starting at letter **a** and going through the alphabet to **z**, you will make quickest progress by writing the letters in family groups as shown below.

I Letters which start with a straight downstroke

*It is important to maintain a pattern with your letters. The round curve at the bottom of letters **l**, **t** and **u** should be similar, and reflect the curve of the letter **o**. The cross-bar of the letter **t** goes just under the upper guideline of the x-height.*

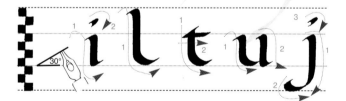

II Letters which start with a downstroke and then arch

*Start the second stroke – the arch – high up on the downstroke. Remember that these letters take their arch shape from that round letter **o**. If you start the second stroke too low on the downstroke then the arch shape does not match the pattern of this alphabet style. The slight upward curve of the exit stroke is made by simply moving your pen in this direction as you take it off the paper. Do not exaggerate this stroke.*
See also page 30 for improving your letters.

*With the letters below, the arch stroke reflects that of the round letter **o**. As a guide, start the second stroke just under the top line for x-height. Keep the last stroke of the letter **k** closer to the downstroke if another letter follows.*

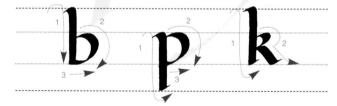

abcdefghijklmnopqrstuvwxyz

4A

Foundational ou Ronde

*Ces lettres sont basées sur celles que l'on retrouve dans les manuscrits anglais du Xe siècle. Ce style est appelé «Foundational», ou Ronde. Dans ce style la lettre **o** est ronde et la plume est tenue à 30° par rapport à l'horizontale. La hauteur d'x est de 4 largeurs de bec. Dessinez une série de lignes directrices parallèles, espacées de 4 largeurs de bec sur un papier lisse adapté et commencez à vous entraîner à tracer les lettres individuelles. Vous ferez des progrès plus rapides en écrivant les lettres de ces familles. Les informations à la page 28 et à la page 30 vous permettront d'améliorer vos lettres.*

I *Lettres commençant par un trait descendant droit. Dessinez vos lettres de manière égale, la courbe arrondie au bas des lettres **l**, **t** et **u** doit être similaire et assortie à la courbe de la lettre **o**. La traverse du **t** se situe juste en dessous de la ligne supérieure de la hauteur d'x.*

II *Lettres commençant par un trait descendant suivi d'un arceau. Commencez le second trait, l'arceau, en haut du trait descendant. La légère courbe montante du trait de sortie s'effectue simplement en déplaçant votre plume dans cette direction tandis que vous la soulevez du papier. Faites le dernier trait de la lettre **k** plus près du trait descendant si une autre lettre suit.*

III *Lettres commençant par un trait incurvé vers la gauche. Ces lettres doivent être rondes et épaisses et le deuxième trait de la lettre **e** ne doit pas être trop bas.*

IV *Lettres diagonales. Le premier trait diagonal est peu profond, ce qui élargit la lettre. À l'exception de la lettre **w**, ces lettres doivent avoir environ la largeur de la lettre **o**.*

V *Lettres qui n'entrent pas dans ces familles. Choisissez les formes les plus simples des lettres **a** et **g** si vous les trouvez plus faciles.*

VI *Chiffres, «et» commercial, et signes de ponctuation.*

Escritura redonda o fundacional

*Esta escritura tiene su origen en los manuscritos escritos en Inglaterra en el siglo X. Este estilo se llama escritura redonda o fundacional o escritura carolina románica minúscula. En este estilo, la letra **o** es redonda y el ángulo de la pluma es 30° con la línea de escritura. El alto de la x es de 4 anchos por altura. Dibuje una serie de líneas guía paralelas a una distancia entre sí de 4 anchos por altura sobre un papel liso y empiece a practicar las letras individualmente. Progresará más rápido escribiendo las letras en estos grupos de familias. Véase información importante para mejorar la escritura en la página 28 y en la página 30.*

I *Letras que empiezan con un trazo vertical recto. Mantenga el mismo patrón para todas las letras. La curva redonda en la base de las letras **l**, **t** y **u** debe ser similar y reflejar la curva de la letra **o**. La tilde de la letra **t** se dibuja justo debajo de la línea de guía superior del alto de la letra x.*

II *Letras que empiezan con un trazo vertical para formar un arco posteriormente. Empiece el segundo trazo, el arco, alto en el trazo vertical. La ligera curvatura hacia arriba del trazo terminal se realiza de forma sencilla moviendo el bolígrafo en esta dirección a medida que lo retira del papel. Mantenga el último trazo de la letra **k** más cerca del vertical si le sigue otra letra.*

III *Letras que empiezan con un trazo curvo hacia la izquierda. Estas letras deben ser redondas y densas y el segundo trazo de la letra **e** no debe ser demasiado bajo.*

IV *Letras diagonales. El primer trazo diagonal es poco profundo lo que hace que la letra sea ancha. Exceptuando la letra **w**, estas letras deben tener el mismo ancho que la letra **o**.*

V *Letras que no encajan en estos grupos de familias. Elija las formas más sencillas de las letras **a** y **g** si le resultan más fáciles.*

VI *Números, signo & y signos de puntuación.*

abcdefghijklmnopqrstuvwxyz

Foundational or Round Hand Majuscules

The majuscules, or capital letters, used with Round Hand are Roman Capitals. These are based on a circle which can be encased within a square. These letters are 6–6·5 nib widths high – that is, less than the heights of the ascenders. The pen nib angle is 30°.

Les majuscules ou lettres capitales, utilisées dans l'écriture Ronde sont des capitales romaines. Elles sont basées sur un cercle qui tient dans un carré. Ces lettres ont une hauteur de 6–6·5 largeurs de bec, inférieure aux hauteurs des ascendantes. L'angle de la plume est de 30°.

Las mayúsculas utilizadas en la escritura redonda son letras románicas mayúsculas. Estas letras se basan en un círculo que puede inscribirse en un cuadrado. Estas letras tienen entre 6–6·5 anchos por altura, lo que es menor que la altura del ascendente. El ángulo de la pluma es de 30°.

A B C D E F G H I

J K L M N O P Q R

S T U V W X Y Z

I Letters based on a round letter O which fits into a square

II Letters which are three-quarters of a square wide

III Letters which are half a square wide

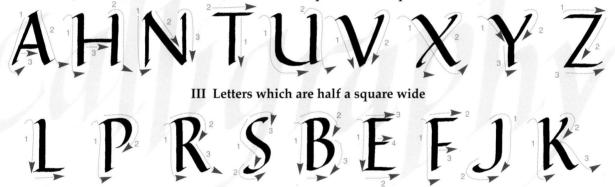

IV Letters which do not fit these families

1 Turn the nib to 60° for the first and third strokes on the letter **N**.

2 Turn the nib to 60° for the first stroke on the letter **M**.

3 Turn the nib to 10° for the diagonal stroke on the letter **Z**.

7

Making a Card Using Foundational Letters

You will need:

- *Stiff card which fits into a suitable envelope when folded in half*
- *Heavy weight white or cream paper*
- *Manuscript coloured ink*
- *Old toothbrush*
- *Old newspapers*
- *Sharp knife and metal straight edge*
- *Wide brush or sponge*
- *Stick or paper glue*
- *Pencil, ruler and dip pen assembled with Round Hand nib such as size 1*

Matériel nécessaire:

- *Carte rigide tenant dans une enveloppe quand elle est pliée en deux*
- *Papier blanc ou crème à fort grammage*
- *Encre de couleur Manuscrit*
- *Brosse à dents usagée*
- *Vieux journaux*
- *Lame tranchante et règle métallique*
- *Pinceau large ou éponge*
- *Bâton de colle ou colle à papier*
- *Porte-mine, règle, porte-plume avec plume Ronde preferée*

Materiales:

- *Cartulina rígida de un tamaño adecuado para introducir en un sobre doblada por la mitad*
- *Papel grueso blanco o crema*
- *Tinta de color para manuscritos*
- *Cepillo de dientes viejo*
- *Periódicos viejos*
- *Cuchillo afilado y regla metálica de borde recto*
- *Pincel ancho o esponja*
- *Barra de pegamento o pegamento para papel*
- *Lapis, regla, portaplumas montada a mano con pluma redonda*

Place a piece of white/cream paper on old newspapers. Dip an old toothbrush in ink, tap it on the edge of the bottle, and then move your forefinger towards you over the bristles to create a spray of dots on the paper.

Placez une feuille de papier blanc/crème sur un vieux journal. Trempez la brosse à dents dans l'encre, frappez-la légèrement sur le bord de la bouteille puis passez l'index à rebrousse-poil, pour moucheter le papier.

Coloque una pieza de papel blanco/crema sobre una hoja de periódico. Unte un cepillo de dientes viejo en la tinta, dé golpecitos con el cepillo en el borde del tintero y seguido empezando por la parte de arriba (hacia usted) pase el dedo índice sobre las cerdas del cepillo para crear un rocío de puntos sobre el papel.

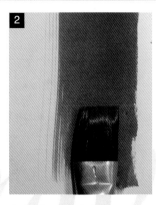

On another sheet of white/cream paper, dip a wide brush or a sponge into Manuscript coloured ink and paint/sponge all over the paper to make it coloured.

Sur une autre feuille de papier blanc/ crème, trempez le pinceau large ou l'éponge dans l'encre de couleur Manuscrit et peignez/ passez l'éponge sur toute la feuille pour la colorer.

En otra hoja de papel blanco/crema, unte un pincel ancho o esponja en la tinta de color para manuscritos y pinte/presione la esponja sobre todo el papel para dar color

Rule up guidelines the correct width apart and practise writing a single letter on a sheet of white or cream paper.

Tracez des lignes directrices espacées de la largeur correcte et entrainez-vous à écrire une seule lettre sur une feuille de papier blanc ou crème.

Trace líneas de guía del ancho correcto y practique escribir una sola letra en una hoja de papel blanco o crema.

Gothic Black Letter Minuscules

III Letters based on the letter o

*Try to make the counters (white space within the letters) similar. The fourth stroke making the bowl of the letter **e** should not be too low, otherwise the letter looks unbalanced.*

IV Letters based on the letter u

*The tail of the letter **y** (and the **g** above) should be kept tight and close into the letter.*

V Letters which do not fit these family groups

*Turn the nib to an angle of 10° for the diagonal stroke

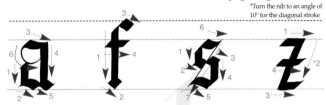

*Choose the simpler form of the letter **a** if you find it easier. In this two-storey letter **a**, the narrow curve is made by using the left-hand corner of the nib – make sure there is sufficient ink in the pen before you do this. The letter **s** has many small strokes!*

****When you have practised these letters you can make them narrower.**

VI Numerals, ampersand and punctuation marks

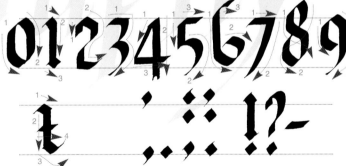

a b c d e f g h i j k l m n o p q r s t u v w x y z

Création d'une carte

Hacer una tarjeta

Choose the best one and cut it out with the knife and straight edge, making a neat square or rectangle. You could do the same with a whole name.

With a knife and straight edge cut out pieces of sprayed, coloured and plain paper that increase by 5mm on each side.

Assemble your card with stick glue. Wipe off any excess.

The finished cards look really professional. You could make matching gift tags, too. Simply make the letter and the patterned and plain pieces of paper smaller, and punch a hole to attach a ribbon.

Choisissez la meilleure et découpez-la avec la lame et la règle, sous forme d'un carré ou d'un rectangle soigné. Vous pouvez faire la même chose avec un nom entier.

À l'aide de la lame et de la règle, découpez des morceaux de papier moucheté, coloré et uni augmenté de 5mm de chaque côté.

Assemblez votre carte avec le bâton de colle, en essuyant l'excédent.

Les cartes finies sont dignes d'un professionnel. Vous pouvez également créer des étiquettes cadeaux assorties. Il vous suffit de diminuer la taille de la lettre et des papiers unis et peints, et de percer un trou pour attacher un ruban.

Elija la más bonita y córtela con el cuchillo y la regla, formando un cuadrado o un rectángulo nítido. Puede hacer lo mismo con todo un nombre.

Utilizando el cuchillo y la regla corte piezas del papel rociado, coloreado y liso con un incremento de 5mm a cada lado

Monte la tarjeta con la barra de pegamento. Limpie el pegamento sobrante.

Las tarjetas acabadas tienen una apariencia muy profesional. También puede hacer etiquetas de regalo a juego. Para ello no tiene más que hacer la letra y las piezas de papel pintadas y lisas más pequeñas y hacer un agujerito para acoplar un lazo.

Spacing *between the strokes* on letters should look about the same as the *spacing between the letters*. It is easy to see this with straight-sided letters (below left). Round and diagonal letters should be slightly closer together to achieve the same evenness (below right).

minim noon

Spacing between words should relate to the letter *o* of that writing style, so there is more space between words for rounder scripts and less space for narrow ones.

nineopenonibs

Spacing between lines should allow for the ascenders and descenders on letter-forms, so they do not clash. Majuscules, or capital letters, can be spaced more closely together because there are no 'tops and tails' to get in the way.

TWENTY SIX LETTERS IN THE ALPHABET finger height

*L'espace **entre les traits** des lettres doit être à peu près le même que l'espace **entre les lettres**. Cela se voit facilement avec les lettres à côté droit (en bas à gauche). Les lettres rondes et les lettres diagonales doivent être légèrement plus proches les unes des autres pour créer la même régularité (en bas à droite).*

*L'espace entre les mots doit être en fonction de la lettre **o** de ce style d'écriture; il y a donc plus d'espace entre les mots pour les écritures plus rondes et moins d'espace pour écritures étroites.*

L'espace entre les lignes doit prendre en compte les ascendantes et les descendants des lettres dessinées, de façon à ne pas se mêler. Les majuscules, ou capitales, peuvent être plus rapprochées car elles n'ont pas de queues gênantes.

*El espaciado **entre los trazos** de las letras debe ser igual que el espaciado **entre las letras**. Esto es fácil de ver con letras rectas (abajo a la izquierda). Las letras redondas y diagonales deberían estar algo más juntas entre sí para lograr la misma uniformidad (abajo a la derecha).*

*El espaciado entre las palabras debe ser en relación con la letra **o** de ese estilo de escritura, por lo tanto hay más espacio entre palabras para escrituras más redondas y menos espacio para tipos de escritura más estrechos.*

El espaciado entre líneas debería ser suficiente para las extensiones ascendentes y descendentes de las formas de las letras de forma que no coincidan. Las letras mayúsculas pueden espaciarse más estrechamente ya que no llevan "gracias" que puedan confluir.

9A

Gothic Black Letter Minuscules

These letters are based on those which were used in manuscripts written in northern Europe from the thirteenth to the fifteenth centuries. They echo the change in architecture to narrow, angular shapes in buildings.

In this style, the letter **o** and all letters are upright, straight-sided and angular. Many of the downstrokes start with diamonds, made by simply moving the nib down and to the right. Because of the lack of curves it can be difficult to identify individual letters when they are written close together. It was during the time of this writing style that the letter *i* was dotted (with a dash) to help legibility.

The x-height for this alphabet is 5 nib widths. Ascenders and descenders are 7 nib widths, and the nib angle 45°. See also key page 28.

I Letters which start with a straight downstroke

Keep your letters upright and the strokes straight. Draw vertical guidelines to help you if you find it difficult to write upright strokes. The crossbar of the letter t goes just under the upper guideline of the x-height.

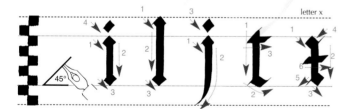

II Letters which start with a downstroke and then 'arch'

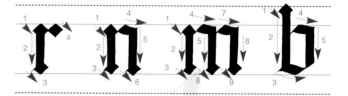

*Try to ensure that the space between the strokes on the letter **n** match that on the letter **m**, and the letter **b**. Let the pen do the work for the fourth stroke on the letter **n** (and similar strokes on other letters); it needs to be straight rather than too curvy.*

*Do not make the sixth stroke on the letter **p** too curved. The fifth stroke on the letter **h** is straight until it almost reaches the base guideline for x-height. Keep the last stroke of the letter **k** closer to the downstroke if another letter follows.*

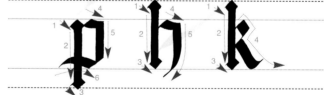

abcdefghijklmnopqrstuvwxyz

10A

Minuscules noires gothiques

*C*es lettres sont basées sur celles des manuscrits rédigés en Europe du nord entre le XIIIe et le XVe siècle. La lettre *o* et toutes les autres lettres sont verticales, à côté droit et angulaires. Beaucoup des traits descendants commencent par des losanges, tracés en déplaçant la plume vers le bas et vers la droite.

La hauteur d'*x* pour cet alphabet est de 5 largeurs de bec. Les ascendantes et les descendantes sont de 7 largeurs de bec, et l'angle de la plume est de 45°. Les informations à la page 28 et à la page 30 vous permettront d'améliorer vos lettres.

I Lettres commençant par un trait descendant droit. Dessinez des lignes directrices verticales pour vous aider si vous trouvez difficile de faire des traits droits. La traverse du *t* se situe juste en dessous de la ligne supérieure de la hauteur d'*x*. L'espace entre les traits doit être régulier et constant. Maintenez le dernier trait de la lettre *k* plus près du trait descendant si une autre lettre suit.

II Lettres commençant par un trait descendant suivi d'un arceau. Veillez à ce que l'espace entre les traits sur la lettre *n* corresponde à celui sur la lettre *m*, et la lettre *b*. Laissez le stylo faire le travail pour le quatrième trait sur la lettre *n* (et traits similaires d'autres lettres); il doit être droite plutôt que trop courbé. Ne pas faire le sixième trait sur la lettre *p* trop courbé. Le cinquième trait sur la lettre *h* est tout droit jusqu'à ce qu'il atteigne la ligne directrice inférieure de la hauteur d'*x*. Maintenez le dernier trait de la lettre *k* plus près du trait descendant si une autre lettre suit.

III Lettres basées sur la lettre *o*. Faites des contrepoinçons (espace blanc à l'intérieur des lettres) similaires. La panse de la lettre *e* ne doit pas être trop basse, sinon la lettre semble déséquilibrée.

IV Lettres basées sur la lettre *u*. La queue de la lettre *y* (et du *g* au-dessus) doit rester serrée dans la lettre.

V Lettres qui n'entrent pas dans ces familles. Pour la lettre *a*, la courbe étroite est tracée en utilisant le coin gauche de la plume – avant de commencer, veillez à ce qu'il y ait suffisamment d'encre dans le porte-plume.

VI Chiffres, «et» commercial, et signes de ponctuation.

***Après vous être entraîné à tracer ces lettres, vous pouvez les faire plus étroites.

Escritura negra gótica minúscula

*E*stas letras se basan en las utilizadas en los manuscritos escritos en el norte de Europa de los siglos XII a XV. La letra *o* y todas las letras son verticales, con lados rectos y angulares. Muchas de las extensiones descendentes empiezan con gracias rómbicas que se dibujan moviendo el plumín hacia abajo y hacia la derecha.

El alto de la letra *x* en este alfabeto es de 5 anchos por altura. Las extensiones ascendentes y descendentes son de 7 anchos por altura y el ángulo de la pluma para esta escritura es 45°. Véase información importante para mejorar la escritura en la página 28 y en la página 30.

I Letras que empiezan con un trazo vertical recto. Dibuje líneas de guía para ayudarle si le resulta difícil dibujar trazos verticales. La tilde de la letra *t* se dibuja justo debajo de la línea de guía superior del alto de la letra *x*. El espacio entre los trazos debe ser igual y uniforme. Mantenga el último trazo de la letra *k* más cerca del trazo vertical si le sigue otra letra.

II Letras que empiezan con un trazo vertical para formar un arco posteriormente. Trate de asegurarse de que el espacio entre los trazos de la letra 'n' coincida con el de la letra 'm' y de la letra 'b'. Que la pluma hacer el trabajo para la trazo de cuarto de la letra 'n' (y los trazos similares en otras letras), sino que debe ser recta y no demasiado curva. No hacer el trazo sexta de la letra 'p' demasiado curvada. El quinta trazo en la letra "h" es recto hasta que casi llegue la línea de guía inferior para la altura de la letra *x*. Mantenga el último trazo de la letra *k* más cerca del trazo vertical si le sigue otra letra.

III Letras basadas en la letra *o*. Haga los contadores (espacio en blanco entre las letras) similares. El espacio interno de la letra *e* no debería ser demasiado bajo, de lo contrario la letra parecería estar desequilibrada.

IV Letras basadas en la letra *u*. La cola de la letra *y* (y de la *g* arriba) deberían estar bastante cerca del cuerpo de la letra.

V Letras que no encajan en estos grupos de familias. La curva estrecha de la letra *a* se dibuja utilizando la esquina izquierda del plumín, compruebe que haya suficiente tinta en el bolígrafo antes de hacer esto.

VI Números, signo & y signos de puntuación.

***Cuando haya practicado estas letras podrá dibujarlas más estrechas.

a b c d e f g h i j k l m n o p q r s t u v w x y z

Gothic Black Letter Majuscules

Majuscules for Gothic Black Letters are taller than the ascenders (the only writing style where this is the case). The letters are decorated with diamonds, flicks, ticks and vertical lines which help to make these large letters hold their own against the density of minuscules.

Les majuscules pour les Lettres noires gothiques sont plus hautes que les ascendantes (seul style d'écriture pour lequel c'est le cas). Les lettres sont décorées de losanges, d'ergots et de lignes verticales qui aident ces grandes lettres à se détacher sur la densité des minuscules.

Las mayúsculas del estilo de escritura negra gótica son más altas que las extensiones ascendentes (el único estilo de escritura que presenta este caso.) Las letras son muy ornamentadas e incluyen gracias rómbicas, florituras, ramitas y líneas verticales que ayudan a que estas letras grandes resalten por su propio mérito contra la densidad de las minúsculas.

I Lettres basées sur une lettre O forme ronde qui s'inscrit dans un carré.
II Lettres larges
III Lettres plus étroites
IV Lettres qui n'entrent pas dans ces familles

I Letters based on a round letter O which fits into a square

I Letras basadas en la letra O que encaja en un cuadrado
II Letras amplias
III Letras más estrechas
IV Letras que no encajan en estos grupos de familias

II Wide letters

III Narrower letters

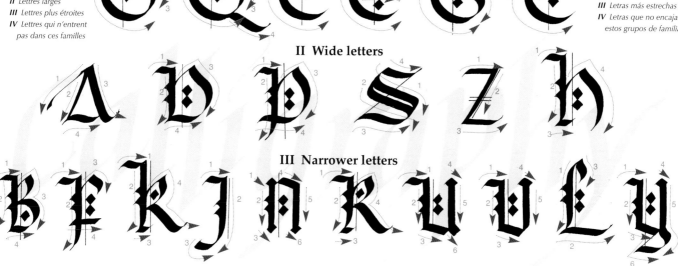

Turn the nib to 10° for the diagonal stroke on the letter **Z**.
Direction arrows and numbers are shown only for the main strokes. Add the diamonds, flicks and straight lines when you have written the letter.

IV Letters which do not fit these families

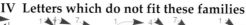

*Pivotez la plume à 10° pour le trait diagonal sur le **Z**.*
Les flèches et les chiffres de direction sont indiqués pour les traits principaux seulement. Ajoutez les losanges, les ergots et les lignes droites après avoir dessiné la lettre.

*Gire el plumín a 10° para dibujar el trazo diagonal de la **Z**.*
Las flechas direccionales y los números solamente se muestran para los trazos principales. Agregue las gracias rómbicas, florituras y líneas rectas cuando haya escrito la letra.

13

Making a bookmark using Gothic Black Letter

You will need:

- Stiff card suitable for a bookmark
- Heavy weight white HP paper (250 gsm+)
- Manuscript coloured and black ink
- Clingfilm or Saranwrap
- Old newspapers
- Sharp knife and metal straight edge
- Wide brush or sponge
- Stick or paper glue
- 3mm wide, 150mm long matching ribbon
- Pencil, ruler and dip pen assembled with Round Hand nib such as size 1

Matériel nécessaire :

- Carte rigide convenant à un signet
- Papier à fort grammage (plus de 250 g/m²)
- Encre noire et encre de couleur Manuscrit
- Film plastique ou cellophane étirable
- Vieux journaux
- Lame tranchante et règle métallique
- Pinceau large ou éponge
- Bâton de colle ou colle à papier
- Ruban assorti de 3mm de large et 150mm de long
- Porte-mine, règle, porte-plume avec plume Ronde preferée

Materiales:

- Cartulina rígida apta para un marcapáginas
- Papel HP grueso (250 g+)
- Tinta para manuscritos de color y negra
- Film transparente o film adherente para envolver alimentos
- Periódicos viejos
- Cuchillo afilado y regla metálica de borde recto
- Pincel ancho o esponja
- Barra de pegamento o pegamento para papel
- Lazo a juego de 3mm de ancho, 150mm de largo
- Lapis, regla, portaplumas montada a mano con pluma redonda

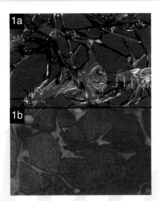

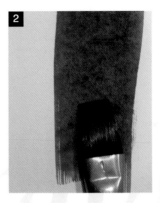

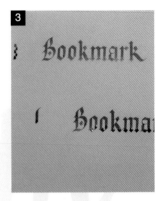

Place a piece of heavy weight paper on old newspapers. Dip a wide brush or sponge in Manuscript coloured ink and paint all over. Quickly tear off a piece of clingfilm and place over the **wet** ink. Pull it together with your fingers. Allow to dry. Remove the clingfilm.

On another sheet of white/cream paper, dip a wide brush or a sponge into Manuscript coloured ink and paint/sponge all over the paper.

Rule up guidelines the correct width apart and practise writing 'Bookmark' on a piece of white paper.

Placez une feuille de papier à fort grammage sur un vieux journal. Trempez le pinceau large ou l'éponge dans l'encre de couleur Manuscrit et peignez tout le papier. Coupez rapidement un morceau de film étirable et posez-le sur l'encre mouillée. Étirez-le avec les doigts. Laissez sécher. Retirez le film étirable.

Sur une autre feuille de papier blanc, trempez le pinceau large ou l'éponge dans l'encre de couleur Manuscrit et peignez/passez l'éponge sur tout le papier.

Tracez des lignes directrices espacées de la largeur correcte et entraînez-vous à écrire 'Signet' sur une feuille de papier blanc.

Coloque una pieza de papel grueso sobre un periódico viejo. Unte un pincel ancho o esponja con tinta de color para manuscritos y pinte todo el papel. Rápidamente, corte un trozo de film transparente y colóquelo sobre la tinta húmeda. Estírelos juntos con los dedos. Deje que la tinta se seque. Quite el film transparente.

En otra hoja de papel blanco, unte un pincel ancho o esponja con la tinta de color para manuscritos y pinte/unte todo el papel con la esponja.

Dibuje líneas de guía del ancho correcto y practique escribir "Bookmark" en una hoja de papel blanco.

Italic Minuscules

III Letters which start with a curved stroke to the left

*The letter **o** is a narrow oval which slants slightly forwards. Notice the counter (white space) which should be upright. Other letters take their shape and form from the letter **o**.*

Turn the nib to an angle of 10° for the diagonal stroke

IV Diagonal letters

The first diagonal stroke is steep. This makes the letter slant slightly forwards.

abcdefghijklmnopqrstuvwxyz

V Letters which do not fit these family groups

*Keep the top and bottom strokes of the letters **f** and **s** flat and open so they do not look like fishhooks! The crossbar of the **f** goes just under the top guideline for x-height. When writing two letters **f** together, combining the first above with the second is often a good choice to avoid clashing base strokes. The middle part of the letter **s** should be a smooth curve; practise making this stroke sinuous to avoid sharp bends or angles. It should be like a swan's neck – no kinks or bumps.*

VI Numerals, ampersand and punctuation marks

Création d'un signet   # Hacer un marcapáginas

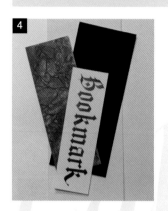

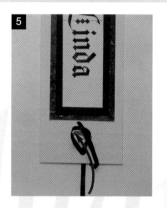

Choose the best one and cut it out with the knife and straight edge. You could do the same with a name. With a knife and straight edge cut out pieces of patterned, coloured and plain paper that increase by 5mm on each side.

Using a hole punch, make a hole in the middle of one end, about 10mm from the edge. Fold the ribbon in half and push it through the hole. Thread through the loose ends as shown and gently pull tight.

You can use up scraps of paper to make your bookmark look even more stylish. Do not waste anything, and do not throw scraps away!

These are bookmarks that people will not want just to leave in a book but have out on show.

Choisissez le plus réussi et découpez-le avec la lame et la règle. Vous pouvez faire la même chose avec un nom. À l'aide de la lame et de la règle, coupez des morceaux de papier à motif, coloré et uni augmenté de 5mm de chaque côté.

Avec une perforatrice, percez un trou central à l'une des extrémités, à environ 10mm du bord. Pliez le ruban en deux et passez-le à travers le trou. Enfilez les extrémités comme sur l'illustration et serrez doucement.

Vous pouvez utiliser des chutes de papier pour rendre votre signet encore plus élégant. Ne gaspillez rien et ne jetez pas les chutes.

Les receveurs de ces signets ne les laisseront pas dans les livres mais voudront les exposer.

Elija la escritura más bonita y córtela con el cuchillo y la regla. Puede hacer lo mismo con un nombre. Utilizando el cuchillo y la regla corte piezas de papel texturado, coloreado y liso con un incremento de 5mm a cada lado.

Utilizando una perforada, haga un agujero en el centro de uno de los extremos a aproximadamente 10mm del borde. Doble el lazo por la mitad e introdúzcalo por el agujero. Enhébrelo a través de los extremos flojos como se muestra y tire con cuidado para apretar el lazo.

También puede utilizar recortes de papel para conferir otra elegancia al marcapáginas. No desperdicie nada ni tire los recortes de papel.

Estos marcapáginas son tan bonitos y elegantes que la gente no querrá guardarlos en un libro sino enseñarlos.

When starting calligraphy is it best to keep to simple layouts as on the left below. Later you can experiment with more exciting ways of placing words and lines. Remember that calligraphy needs room to breathe – leave wide margins. Artworks can, of course, be landscape as well as portrait.

Pour débuter, il est toujours plus simple de commencer par une simple mise en page comme celle ci-dessous à gauche. Après, vous pourrez laisser aller votre imaginaire dans des mises en page plus complexes. Souvenez-vous que la calligraphie a besoin d'espace pour respirer. Laisser de larges marges. Vos créations peuvent-être au format paysage comme portrait.

Al iniciar la caligrafía es mejor mantener los diseños simples como abajo a la izquierda. Más tarde, puede experimentar con formas más emocionantes de la colocación de palabras y líneas. Recuerde que la caligrafía necesita espacio para respirar - dejar márgenes amplios. Obras pueden, por supuesto, ser paisaje, así como retrato.

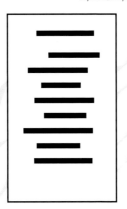

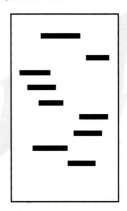

Aligned left pieces are easiest to write out.	*Centred pieces often draw the eye to the shape the lines make.*	*Lines written around a central, vertical line need to be balanced and have a spine.*	*Avoid placing the lines so that there is no spine. Also try to avoid diagonals.*	*Bottom heavy pieces do not always work. Top heavy are often even worse!*
Les textes alignés à gauche sont les plus faciles.	*Les textes centrés attirent l'œil de part la construction des lignes.*	*Les lignes écrites autour d'une ligne centrale doivent être équilibrées symétriquement.*	*Il faut bien faire attention à ne pas placer les lignes sans symétrie. Evitez aussi les diagonales.*	*Les caractères de grandes tailles placés en bas des œuvres ne fonctionnent pas toujours. En haut, c'est encore pire!*
Alineados pedazos izquierdos son más fáciles de escribir.	*Piezas centrados a menudo atraen la mirada a la construcción de las líneas.*	*Las líneas escritas en torno a una línea central vertical tienen que haber un equilibrio simétrico.*	*No coloque las líneas de modo que no sean simétricas.También evite las diagonales.*	*Piezas que son pesados en la parte inferior no siempre funcionan. Piezas que son pesadas en la parte superior son peores!*

Italic Minuscules

Italic letters were developed in Italy (hence the name) in the fourteenth and fifteenth centuries by the humanists.

In this style, the letter **o** is narrow, oval and slanting, and all the letters take their form from this. Hold your nib at an angle of 45° to the horizonal for these letters.

The x-height for this alphabet is 5 nib widths and ascenders and descenders are long and elegant at 8 nib widths. With a pencil and long ruler draw a series of parallel guidelines which are 5 nib widths apart on suitable smooth paper and start to practise the individual letters. You will make quickest progress by writing the letters in family groups as below. See also key page 29.

I Letters which start with a downstroke

*The lower curves of Italic are significant for this writing style. They are smooth, not sharp or angular; there is also almost a slight pause before making the upstroke. The entry stroke is a simple curve, made naturally by the pen nib. As with most writing styles, the crossbar of the letter **t** is just below the top line for x-height. Take the pressure off the pen, and push the first stroke of the letter **u** right up to the top guideline for x-height to achieve that smooth inner curve – if you stop you won't get this shape.*

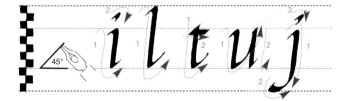

II Letters which start with a downstroke and then arch

*As with the letter **u**, the smooth inner curve of the letters in this family is made by taking the pressure off the pen and pushing the pen nib from the base guideline for x-height right up to the upper guideline for x-height. If you stop halfway, it is very difficult to avoid an obvious angular join and you are not able to achieve this lovely curve. Notice particularly the 'counter' – the smooth white space within the letters.*

*The second stroke for these letters should start at the base guideline for x-height and should start to move away from the downstroke about mid-way between the two guidelines for x-height. The third stroke of the letters **b** and **p** starts at the base guideline for x-height and curves gently upwards.*

abcdefghijklmnopqrstuvwxyz

Minuscules italiques

*L*es lettres italiques ont été développées en Italie (d'où leur nom) par les humanistes des XIVe et XVe siècles.

Dans ce style, la lettre *o* est étroite, ovale et inclinée. L'angle de la plume est de 45° et la hauteur d'*x* est de 5 largeurs de bec avec des ascendantes et des descendantes de 8 largeurs de bec. Dessinez des lignes directrices parallèles espacées de 5 largeurs de bec sur un papier lisse adéquat et commencez à vous entraîner à tracer les lettres individuelles. Vous ferez des progrès plus rapides en écrivant les lettres de ces familles, tel que ci-dessous. Les informations à la page 29 et à la page 31 vous permettront d'améliorer vos lettres.

I **Lettres commençant par un trait descendant.** *Ce style d'écriture se caractérise par des courbes inférieures régulières, sans angles ni arêtes vives. Les traits d'entrée sont de simples courbes. La traverse du* t *se situe juste en dessous de la ligne supérieure de la hauteur d'*x. *Relâchez la pression sur la plume et poussez le premier trait de la lettre* u *jusqu'en haut de la ligne supérieure pour la hauteur d'*x, *sans vous arrêter, pour réussir cette courbe intérieure régulière.*

II **Lettres commençant par un trait descendant suivi d'un arceau.** *Les deuxièmes traits pour ces lettres doivent commencer au niveau de la ligne directrice inférieure de la hauteur d'*x *et doivent s'éloigner du trait descendant environ au milieu, entre les deux lignes directrices de la hauteur d'*x.

III **Lettres commençant par un trait incurvé vers la gauche.** *La lettre* o *est un ovale étroit légèrement incliné vers l'avant. Notez le contrepoinçon (espace blanc) qui doit être droit. La forme et le dessin des autres lettres découlent de la lettre* o.

IV **Lettres diagonales.** *Le premier trait diagonal est fortement penché, ce qui incline la lettre légèrement vers l'avant.*

V **Lettres qui n'entrent pas dans ces familles.** *Gardez les traits inférieurs et supérieurs des lettres* f *et* s *plats et ouverts de façon à ce qu'ils ne ressemblent pas à des hameçons! La traverse du* f *se situe juste en dessous de la ligne supérieure de la hauteur d'*x.

VI **Chiffres, «et» commercial et signes de ponctuation.**

Itálicas minúsculas

*L*a escritura itálica fue desarrollada en Italia (de ahí su nombre) en los siglos XIV y XV por los humanistas.

En este estilo de escritura la letra *o* es estrecha, ovalada e inclinada. El ángulo de la pluma para la letra itálica es 45° y la altura de la *x* es de 5 anchos por altura mientras que la altura de los ascendentes y los descendentes es de 8 anchos por altura. Dibuje líneas de guía paralelas a una distancia de 5 anchos sobre un papel liso apto y empiece a practicar las letras individualmente. Progresará más rápido escribiendo las letras en grupos de familias como se indica abajo. Véase información importante para mejorar la escritura en la página 29 y en la página 31.

I **Letras que empiezan con un trazo vertical.** *Para este estilo de escritura las curvas inferiores suaves, sin ser agudas o angulares, son importantes. Los trazos de comienzo son sencillas curvas. La tilde de la letra* t *se dibuja justo debajo de la línea superior de la altura de la letra* x. *Sin ejercer presión con la pluma empuje el primer trazo de la letra* u *hacia arriba hasta la parte superior de la línea de guía para la altura de la letra* x *sin parar para lograr una curva interna fluida.*

II **Letras que empiezan con un trazo vertical para formar un arco posteriormente.** *Los segundos trazos para estas letras deben empezarse en la base de la línea de guía para la altura de la letra* x *y deben empezar a alejarse del trazo vertical aproximadamente en la sección central de las dos líneas de guía para la altura de la letra* x.

III **Letras que empiezan con un trazo curvo hacia la izquierda.** *La letra* o *es un óvalo estrecho que se inclina ligeramente hacia delante. Obsérvese el contador (espacio en blanco) que debe ser recto. Otras letras toman su forma de la letra* o.

IV **Letras diagonales.** *El primer trazo diagonal es agudo lo que hace que la letra se incline ligeramente hacia delante.*

V **Letras que no encajan en estos grupos de familias.** *Mantenga los trazos superiores e inferiores de las letras* f *y* s *lisos y abiertos para que no parezcan anzuelos de pesca. La tilde de la* f *se dibuja justo debajo de la línea de guía superior para la altura de la letra* x.

VI **Números, signo & y signos de puntuación**

a b c d e f g h i j k l m n o p q r s t u v w x y z

Italic Majuscules

The Majuscules, or capital letters, used with Italic letters can be Roman Capitals, but with a slight forward slant, or Roman Capitals that are a little narrower, as here. Letters are 7 nib widths high – that is, less than the heights of the ascenders. The pen nib angle is the same as for minuscules – 45°.

Les majuscules ou les capitales, utilisées avec des lettres italiques, peuvent être des capitales romaines, mais avec une légère inclinaison vers l'avant, ou des capitales romaines qui sont un peu plus étroites, comme ici. Les lettres sont hautes de 7 largeurs de bec, à savoir inférieures aux hauteurs des ascendantes. L'angle de la plume est de 45°, comme pour les minuscules.

Las letras mayúsculas utilizadas en la escritura itálica pueden ser romanas mayúsculas, pero con una ligera inclinación hacia delante o románicas mayúsculas un poco más estrechas, como se muestra aquí. Las letras son de 7 anchos por altura, que es menos que las alturas de los ascendentes. El ángulo de la pluma es 45°, igual que para las minúsculas.

I Letters based on an oval letter *O*

I Lettres basées sur une letter **O** forme ovale

II Lettres avec une largeur de trois quarts de la lettre **O**

III Lettres étroites

IV Lettres qui n'entrent pas dans ces familles

I Letras basadas en la letra **O** ovalada

II Letras que tienen una anchura de tres cuartos de la letra **O**

III Letras estrechas

IV Letras que no encajan en estos grupos de familias

II Letters which are three-quarters of the width of the letter *O*

III Narrow letters

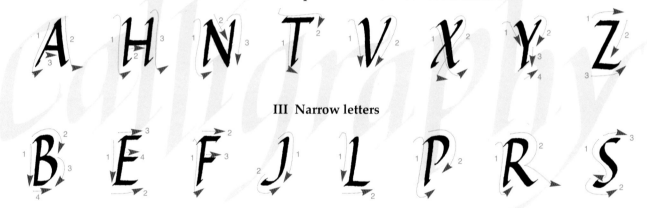

IV Letters which do not fit these families

1 Turn the nib to 60° for the first and third strokes on the letter **N**.

2 Turn the nib to 60° for the first stroke on the letter **M**.

3 Turn the nib to 10° for the diagonal stroke on the letter **Z**.

1 Pivotez la plume à 60° pour le premier trait et le troisième trait de la lettre **N**.

2 Pivotez la plume à 60° pour les premiers traits de la lettre **M**.

3 Pivotez la plume à 10° pour le trait diagonal de la lettre **Z**.

1 Gire el plumín a 60° para el primer y el tercer trazo de la letra **N**.

2 Gire el plumín a 60° para los primeros trazos de la letra **M**.

3 Gire el plumín a 10° para el trazo diagonal de la letra **Z**.

19

A Wedding Invitation Using Italic

You will need:

- *Good quality white paper*
- *Manuscript black ink*
- *Sharp pencil*
- *Good quality 00 paintbrush or fine technical pen*
- *Sharp knife and metal straight edge*
- *Stick or paper glue*
- *Photocopier or scanner and printer*
- *Pencil, ruler and dip pen assembled with Round Hand nib such as sizes 3 and 4*

This is the process whenever you need more than one invitation.

Matériel nécessaire :

- *Papier blanc de bonne qualité*
- *Encre noire Manuscrit*
- *Crayon pointu*
- *Pinceau 00 ou stylo technique fin de bonne qualité*
- *Lame tranchante et règle métallique*
- *Bâton de colle ou colle à papier*
- *Photocopieuse ou scanneur et imprimante*
- *Porte-mine, règle, porte-plume avec plume Ronde preferée*

Procédé à utiliser s'il vous faut plus d'une invitation.

Materiales:

- *Papel blanco de buena calidad*
- *Tinta negra para manuscritos*
- *Lapicero afilado*
- *Pincel 00 de buena calidad o bolígrafo técnico fino*
- *Cuchillo afilado y regla metálica de borde recto*
- *Barra de pegamento o pegamento para papel*
- *Fotocopiadora o escáner e impresora*
- *Lapis, regla, portaplumas montada a mano con pluma redonda*

Este es el procedimiento siempre que necesite más de una invitación.

1

Mr and Mrs Frederick Hintze

Mr Daniel Jones   Rachel Joann

request the pleasure of your company

at the marriage of their daughter

at St Luke's Church, Weald   on 18th March at

and afterwards at The Glebe House

to   RSVP: The Glebe House · Weald · Surrey

Decide on your text. Rule up guide-lines the correct width apart and write out the text. You may choose to write some parts of the invitation smaller, in which case rule up guidelines appropriately.

Décidez du texte. Tracez des lignes directrices espacées de la largeur correcte et écrivez votre texte. Vous pouvez choisir d'écrire plus petit sur certaines parties de l'invitation, dans quel cas tracez les lignes directrices en conséquence.

Elija el texto. Dibuje líneas de guía del ancho correcto y escriba el texto. Quizá prefiera escribir algunas secciones de la invitación más pequeñas, en cuyo caso dibuje las líneas de guía necesarias.

2

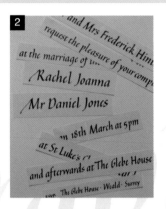

It does not matter if you make a mistake, simply rewrite the letter. Cut out and tape together all the best letters and words, and place them carefully on a piece of paper.

Si vous vous trompez, ce n'est pas grave, il vous suffit d'écrire la lettre à nouveau. Découpez et collez ensemble toutes les lettres et tous les mots les plus réussis et placez-les soigneusement sur une feuille de papier.

No importa si comete un error, sencillamente vuelva a escribir la letra. Corte y pegue juntas las letras y las palabras más bonitas y colóquelas con cuidado sobre una hoja de papel.

3

Rule up three vertical guidelines 120mm long and 5mm apart. Mark points at 10mm intervals. Draw a wavy line as a stem, and then add side branches. Draw circles as guides for flowers, add leaves. With a brush or fine pen, ink in.

Tracez trois lignes directrices verticales de 120mm de long, espacées de 5mm. Faites des points de repère à 10mm d'intervalle. Dessinez une ligne ondulée représentant une tige puis ajoutez des branches sur les côtés. Dessinez des cercles comme guides pour les fleurs et les feuilles. Encrez à l'aide d'un pinceau ou d'un stylo fin.

Dibuje tres líneas de guía verticales de 120mm de largo y 5mm de separación. Marque puntos a intervalos de 10mm. Dibuje una línea ondulada en forma de tallo y agregue ramitas laterales. Dibuje círculos como guías para flores. Rellene de tinta con un pincel o bolígrafo fino.

Uncials

These letters are based on those which were used in manuscripts written in England in the late seventh and early eighth century. The ones here are copied from a tiny manuscript reputed to have been found in Northumberland in the tomb of St Cuthbert – a famous English saint. The book is now in the British Library.

The letters are round and grand, with a small x-height of three-and-a-half nib widths, which makes them look chunky. Although there are a few ascenders and descenders which just extend to five-and-a-half nib widths each, it is essentially a majuscule writing style. The nib is held at an angle of 30°, the same as Round Hand or Foundational letters.

I Letters which start with a straight downstroke

Use simple entry and exit curved strokes, and try not to exaggerate them too much – the pen does all the work. Not exaggerating is especially true of the second stroke on the letter T. Make slight movements to the left as you start and end this stroke, and keep the main part straight.

II Letters which start with a downstroke and then arch

Remember that the letter o is round, and ensure that the bowls of the letters h and p keep that roundness – do not put your letters on a diet! Start the bowl high up on the downstroke so that the shape of the arch reflects the shape of the letter o.

With these letters, too, the arch stroke reflects that of the round letter o. As a guide start the second stroke just under the top line for x-height. Keep the last stroke of the letter k closer to the downstroke if another letter follows.

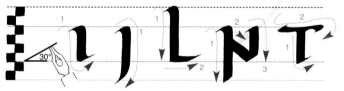

a b c d e f g h i j k l m n o p q r s t u v w x y z

22A

Flourishes Fioritures Ornamentación

The most important aspect to remember about flourishing letters is that the essence of the letter stays the same, and the flourishing is on the periphery, as you can see below. Do not be tempted to distort the letter-shapes when flourishing.

Most ascenders can be flourished in a similar way to the letter *h* below, and most descenders as in the letters *f* and *y*.

Flourishes add emphasis, and that does not occur if you use too many. Remember – flourish little, but flourish well.

Invitation de mariage Invitación de boda

4

5

6

7

Cut out the design and place with the written text. Decide on the margins for the card, being generous with them – calligraphy needs room to breathe!

On a sheet of paper, mark a vertical left margin and paste the design about 25mm from this. Mark another vertical line 15mm from the design and paste on the text in the correct order, making sure the lines are straight.

Photocopy the invitations on to good quality card, or get them professionally printed.

Once printed, the invitations look very impressive.

Découpez le dessin et placez-le par rapport au texte écrit. Décidez de la taille des marges pour la carte – soyez généreux car la calligraphie a besoin de place pour s'exprimer!

Sur une feuille de papier, repérez une marge verticale gauche et collez le dessin à environ 25mm de cette marge. Repérez une autre ligne verticale à 15mm du dessin et collez le texte dans l'ordre correct, en veillant à ce que les lignes soient bien droites.

Photocopiez les invitations sur de la cartoline de bonne qualité ou faites-les imprimer par un professionnel.

Une fois imprimées, ces invitations font énormément d'effet.

Corte el diseño y colóquelo con el texto escrito. Cuando decida el tamaño de los márgenes de la tarjeta sea generoso, la caligrafía necesita espacio para respirar.

En una hoja de papel, marque el margen vertical izquierdo y pegue el diseño a una distancia de 25mm del margen. Marque otra línea vertical a una distancia de 15mm del diseño y pegue el texto en el orden correcto, comprobando que las líneas estén rectas

Fotocopie las invitaciones utilizando cartulina de buena calidad o imprímalas profesionalmente.

Una vez impresas las invitaciones quedan muy atractivas y elegantes.

21

III Letters which start with a curved stroke to the left

*These letters should be round and fat. The third stroke making the bowl of the letter **e** should not be too low, otherwise the letter looks unbalanced.*

IV Diagonal letters

*Turn the nib to an angle of 10° for the diagonal stroke

*The first diagonal stroke is quite shallow. This makes the letter wide. Apart from the letter **w**, these letters should be about the width of the letter **o**.*

V Letters which do not fit these family groups

*Make the diagonal stroke on the letter **a** smooth and clean. The bowl should not extend beyond the mid-way point between the top and base guidelines for x-height. Keep the curves of the letters **s** smooth and sinuous. Keep the last stroke of the letter **k** closer to the downstroke if another letter follows.*

VI Numerals, ampersand and punctuation marks

a b c d e f ʒ h ı j k l ɱ n o p q ʀ s т u v w x y z

Onciales

Ces lettres sont basées sur celles qui étaient utilisées dans les manuscrits anglais de la fin du VIIe, début du VIIIe siècle. Les lettres sont rondes, avec une hauteur d'x de 3·5 largeurs de bec; les ascendantes et les descendantes atteignent chacune 5·5 largeurs de bec. L'angle de la plume est de 30°. Les informations à la page 29 et à la page 31 vous permettront d'améliorer vos lettres.

I *Lettres commençant par un trait descendant droit. Utilisez de simples traits incurvés d'entrée et de sortie. N'exagérez pas le deuxième trait sur la lettre **T**. Faites de légers mouvements vers la gauche lorsque vous commencez et finissez ce trait et gardez la partie principale droite.*

II *Lettres commençant par un trait descendant suivi d'un arceau. La lettre **o** est ronde, harmonisée par les lettres **h** et **p**. Commencez la panse en haut du trait descendant de façon à ce que la forme de l'arceau reflète la lettre **o**. À titre de guide pour la forme de l'arceau, commencez le deuxième trait juste en dessous de la ligne supérieure de la hauteur d'x. Faites le dernier trait de la lettre **k** plus près du trait descendant si une autre lettre suit.*

III *Lettres commençant par un trait incurvé vers la gauche. Ces lettres doivent être rondes. La panse de la lettre **e** ne doit pas être trop basse, sinon la lettre paraîtra déséquilibrée.*

IV *Lettres diagonales. Le premier trait diagonal est peu profond, ce qui élargit la lettre. À l'exception de la lettre **w**, ces lettres doivent avoir environ la largeur de la lettre **o**.*

V *Lettres qui n'entrent pas dans ces familles. Le trait diagonal de la lettre **a** doit être régulier et soigné. La panse ne doit pas dépasser la mi-distance. Les courbes de la lettre **s** sont souples et régulières. Faites le dernier trait de la lettre **k** plus près du trait descendant si une autre lettre suit.*

VI *Chiffres, «et» commercial et signes de ponctuation.*

Unciales

Estas letras se basan en las utilizadas en los manuscritos escritos en Inglaterra a finales del siglo XVII y principios del siglo XVIII. Las letras son redondas con un ancho por altura de la letra x de 3·5 anchos; los ascendentes y los descendentes se extienden a 5·5 anchos por altura cada uno. El ángulo de la pluma para la letra uncial es de 30°. Véase información importante para mejorar la escritura en la página 29 y en la página 31.

I *Letras que empiezan con un trazo vertical recto. Utilice trazos curvos de comienzo y terminación sencillos. No exagere el segundo trazo de la letra **T**. Realice movimientos ligeros hacia la izquierda según empieza y termina este trazo y mantenga la parte principal recta.*

II *Letras que empiezan con un trazo vertical para formar un arco posteriormente. La letra **o** es redonda y las letras **h** y **p** reflejan esta redondez. Empiece el espacio interno alto en el trazo vertical de forma que la forma del arco refleje la forma de la letra **o**. Como guía para la forma del arco empiece el segundo trazo justo debajo de la línea superior para la altura de la letra x. Mantenga el último trazo de la letra **k** más cerca del trazo vertical si le sigue otra letra.*

III *Letras que empiezan con un trazo curvo hacia la izquierda. Estas letras deben ser redondas. El espacio interno de la letra **e** no debe ser demasiado bajo, de lo contrario la letra parecerá estar desequilibrada.*

IV *Letras diagonales. El primer trazo diagonal es poco profundo lo que hace que la letra sea ancha. Exceptuando la letra **w**, estas letras deben tener el mismo ancho que la letra **o**.*

V *Letras que no encajan en estos grupos de familias. Dibuje el trazo diagonal de la letra fluido y limpio. El espacio interno no debe extenderse más allá del punto central. Las curvas de las letras **s** son suaves y sinuosas. Mantenga el último trazo de la letra **k** más cerca del trazo vertical si le sigue otra letra.*

VI *Números, signo & y signos de puntuación.*

a b c d e f g h i j k l m n o p q r s t u v w x y z

Creating an artwork in Uncials

You will need:

- Two sheets of good quality smooth paper of a suitable size for the finished text
- Layout paper or similar for roughs
- 5mm of gouache (Calligraphy Gouache if possible), mixed to a thin, runny cream with water and an old brush
- Sharp pencil
- Sticks of suitable coloured Conté pastels (not oil pastels) a knife and small dishes
- Cotton wool pads or balls
- Sharp knife and metal straight edge
- Masking or magic tape
- Pencil, ruler and dip pen assembled with Round Hand nib such as size 2 and 3

Matériel nécessaire :

- Deux feuilles de papier lisse de bonne qualité d'un format adapté au texte fini.
- Papier translucide ou similaire pour les brouillons
- 5mm de gouache mélangée au pinceau avec de l'eau pour obtenir une consistance liquide et crémeuse
- Crayon pointu
- Bâtonnets de pastels de couleur Conté (pas de pastels à l'huile), une lame et des petites coupelles
- Disques ou boules de coton hydrophile
- Lame tranchante et règle métallique
- Ruban de masquage ou ruban adhésif invisible
- Porte-mine, règle, porte-plume avec plume Ronde preferée

Materiales:

- Dos hojas de papel liso y suave de buena calidad de un tamaño apto para el texto acabado.
- Papel de calco o similar para borradores
- 5mm de aguada mezclada con agua para formar una crema delgada y suelta, y un pincel
- Lapicero afilado
- Pinturas pastel Conte de los colores deseados (no pasteles al óleo) un cuchillo y cuencos pequeños
- Bolas o torundas de algodón
- Cuchillo afilado y regla metálica de borde recto
- Cinta adhesiva protectora o invisible.
- Lapis, regla, portaplumas montada a mano con pluma redonda

1

Decide on your text. Rule up guidelines the correct width apart and write out the text. It does not matter if you make a mistake, simply rewrite the letter.

Décidez de votre texte. Tracez des lignes directrices espacées de la largeur correcte et rédigez le texte. Si vous vous trompez, ce n'est pas grave, écrivez la lettre à nouveau.

Elija el texto. Dibuje las líneas de guía al ancho correcto y escriba el texto elegido. No importa si comete un error, sencillamente vuelva a escribir la letra

2

Cut out all the best letters and words, and place them carefully on a piece of paper.

Découpez toutes les lettres et tous les mots les plus réussis et placez-les soigneusement sur une feuille de papier.

Corte las letras y palabras más bonitas y colóquelas con cuidado sobre una hoja de papel.

3

Consider the text, and decide which words or phrases should be enlarged for emphasis. Rewrite these with a larger nib, having ruled guidelines at the correct height.

Décidez quels mots ou quelles phrases dans votre texte vous allez agrandir pour les mettre en évidence. Écrivez-les à nouveau avec une plume plus large entre des lignes directrices de la hauteur correcte.

Observe el texto y decida las palabras y frases que deberían ser más alargadas para resaltar el texto. Vuelva a escribirlas con un plumín más grande y las líneas de guía del ancho correcto.

Création artistique

Crear una obra de arte

Experiment with the position of the words on the page. Here the text is aligned left.

Essayez diverses dispositions des mots sur la page. Ici le texte est aligné à gauche.

Pruebe colocar las palabras en posiciones distintas en la página. Aquí, el texto está alineado a la izquierda.

The text here is centred. Notice that visually you are aware of the shape the lines make.

Ici le texte est centré. Vous remarquerez que vous êtes sensible visuellement à la forme créée par les lignes.

El texto aquí está centrado. Observe que visualmente se nota a simple vista la forma que toman las líneas.

The text here is ranged badly around a central line. It is important that there is a spine and the lines overlap at some point in the middle, or the piece falls apart. Try also to avoid the start and ends of three or more lines making a diagonal.

Le texte ici est mal disposé par rapport à une ligne centrale. Il est important d'avoir une épine dorsale et des lignes qui se chevauchent en un point médian, sinon l'effet n'est pas réussi. Essayez également d'éviter le début et la fin de trois lignes ou plus formant une diagonale.

El texto en este ejemplo está mal dispuesto en torno a una línea central. Es importante que haya un esqueleto y que las líneas se solapen en algún punto en el centro o la composición quedará fea. Así mismo, procure evitar que el principio y la terminación de tres o más líneas formen una diagonal

When you have selected the arrangements which you like best, ensure that the spaces between lines are at equal distances, and use tiny pieces of masking or magic tape to secure the lines to the paper.

Après avoir sélectionné les dispositions que vous préférez, assurez-vous que les lignes sont espacées de manière égale, et utilisez de petits morceaux de ruban de masquage ou de ruban adhésif invisible pour fixer les lignes sur le papier.

Cuando haya seleccionado la composición o composiciones que más le gusten, compruebe que el espaciado entre las líneas sea igual y utilice trocitos pequeños de cinta adhesiva para pegar las líneas sobre el papel.

25

Creating an artwork in Uncials (continued)

8

9

10

11

Guard sheet

Using a pencil and a ruler, measure the distances between the lines and also the line lengths; record where each line starts and ends.

Place the taped text strips on their sheet of paper on to a sheet of good quality smooth paper. The latter should be at least 30mm larger all round to allow for good margins. Move around for the best position.

Using a sharp pencil make a tiny mark on the good quality paper to indicate where the text begins, and then with a pencil and ruler transfer the measurements you have taken from your rough layout, and rule faint pencil lines.

Carefully lift the first line of text from your rough layout and, with tiny pieces of masking or magic tape, attach it to the good quality paper just above the ruled first line. Copy the text. Repeat this for all the lines.

À l'aide d'un crayon et d'une règle, mesurez les distances entre les lignes ainsi que la longueur des lignes; notez où commence et finit chaque ligne.

Placez les bandes de textes collées sur leur papier par le ruban sur une feuille de papier lisse de bonne qualité. Prévoyez au moins 30mm de plus tout autour pour avoir de bonnes marges. Essayez plusieurs dispositions pour trouver la meilleure.

Faites une petite marque avec le crayon pointu sur le papier de bonne qualité pour indiquer où le texte commence, puis avec le crayon et la règle transférez les mesures que vous avez prises sur votre brouillon et tracez des lignes légères au crayon.

Soulevez délicatement la première ligne de texte de votre brouillon et, à l'aide de très petits morceaux de ruban de masquage ou de ruban adhésif invisible, fixez-la sur votre papier de bonne qualité, juste au-dessus de la première ligne tracée. Copiez le texte. Répétez cela pour toutes les lignes.

Utilizando un lápiz y una regla, mida la distancia entre las líneas y la largura de las líneas; marque el principio y el final de cada línea.

Coloque las tiras de texto con cinta adhesiva sobre una hoja de papel liso de buena calidad. La hoja de papel debe ser al menos 30mm más grande por todo su alrededor para que quede un margen bonito. Mueva las tiras de texto hasta lograr la mejor posición.

Utilizando un lapicero afilado haga una marquita en el papel de buena calidad para indicar el principio del texto y luego con el lápiz y la regla transfiera las medidas que ha tomado del borrador y dibuje líneas a lápiz pero sin marcar mucho.

Con cuidado levante la primera línea de texto del borrador y con trocitos de cinta adhesiva invisible péguela sobre el papel de buena calidad justo encima de la primera línea. Copie el texto. Repita esto para las otras líneas.

Création artistique   Crear una obra de arte

12

13

14

15

Decide on the best colours of pastel which suit your chosen text. With a dull blade, scrape powder from the pastel into a saucer/palette. Repeat this for a limited number of related colours. Dip a cotton wool pad into the powder and press it into the paper.

Add additional colours if you think this is appropriate, but do not add too many colours so your work looks garish.

It is rare that everything works the first time, and so repeat it all on the second sheet of paper adjusting colour and the position of lines if necessary.

The finished piece of artwork is good enough to put in a frame and hang on a wall.

Décidez des couleurs de pastels qui conviennent le mieux au texte que vous avez choisi. Avec une lame émoussée, raclez la poudre des pastels dans une soucoupe/palette. Répétez cela pour quelques couleurs assorties. Trempez un disque de coton hydrophile dans la poudre et pressez dans le papier.

Ajoutez des couleurs supplémentaires, si vous le jugez bon, mais pas trop sinon votre travail sera criard.

Il est rare de réussir au premier essai donc recommencez le tout sur la seconde feuille de papier, en ajustant la couleur et la position des lignes au besoin.

L'œuvre obtenue est d'une qualité digne d'être encadrée et accrochée au mur.

Decida los colores pastel que mejor encajen con el texto elegido. Utilizando una cuchilla roma, raspe polvo de la pintura pastel en un platillo/paleta. Repita esto con varios colores (pero sin ser muchos) que coordinen bien. Unte una bolita de algodón en el polvo y presione el algodón sobre el papel.

Agregue otros colores si lo considera apropiado, pero sin añadir muchos colores diferentes para que la obra no quede demasiado chillona.

Es raro que todo quede bien a la primera por ello repita el proceso en la segunda hoja de papel y ajuste el color y la posición de las líneas según el gusto.

La obra de arte acabada quedará preciosa enmarcada y colgada de una pared.

Alphabets – key information

Foundational or Round Hand

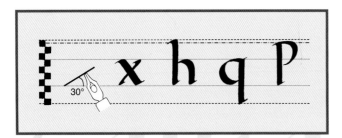

- *x-height – 4 nib widths, ascenders 7 nib widths, descenders 7 nib widths*
- *height of majuscules (capitals) – 6·5 nib widths*
- *nib angle – 30°*
- *slant – upright*
- *letter o form – round*
- *serifs – simple entry and exit strokes*

FOUNDATIONAL OU RONDE
- *hauteur d'x de 4 largeurs de bec, ascendantes de 7 largeurs de bec, descendantes de 7 largeurs de bec*
- *hauteur des majuscules (capitales) – 6·5 largeurs de bec*
- *angle de la plume – 30°*
- *lettre o de forme – ronde*
- *inclinaison – droite*
- *empattements – traits simples d'entrée et de sortie*

FUNDACIONAL O REDONDA
- *altura de la x 4 anchos por altura, ascendentes 7 anchos por altura, descendentes 7 anchos por altura*
- *altura de las mayúsculas – 6·5 anchos por altura*
- *ángulo de la pluma – 30°*
- *la forma de la letra o – redonda*
- *inclinada – recta*
- *gracias – trazos sencillos de comienzo y terminación*

Gothic Black Letter

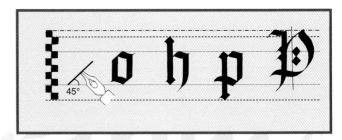

- *x-height – 5 nib widths, ascenders 7 nib widths, descenders 7 nib widths*
- *height of majuscules (capitals) – 8 nib widths*
- *nib angle – 45°*
- *slant – upright*
- *letter o form – angular*
- *serifs – diamonds*

LETTRES NOIRES GOTHIQUES
- *hauteur d'x de 5 largeurs de bec, ascendantes de 7 largeurs de bec, descendantes de 7 largeurs de bec*
- *hauteur des majuscules (capitales) – 8 largeurs de bec*
- *angle de la plume – 45°*
- *lettre o de forme – angulaire*
- *inclinaison – droite*
- *empattements – losanges*

LETRA NEGRA GÓTICA
- *altura de la x 5 anchos por altura, ascendentes 7 anchos por altura, descendentes 7 anchos por altura*
- *altura de las mayúsculas – 8 anchos por altura*
- *ángulo de la pluma – 45°*
- *la forma de la letra o – angular*
- *inclinada – recta*
- *gracias – rómbicas*

Italic

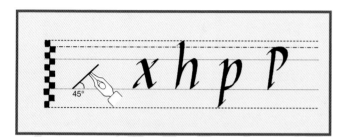

Uncial

- *x-height – 5 nib widths, ascenders 8 nib widths, descenders 8 nib widths*
- *height of majuscules (capitals) – 7 nib widths*
- *nib angle – 45°*
- *slant – 5° approximately*
- *letter **o** form – forward slanting oval*
- *serifs – simple entry and exit strokes*

ITALIQUES

- *hauteur d'x – 5 largeurs de bec, ascendantes de 8 largeurs de bec, descendantes de 8 largeurs de bec*
- *hauteur des majuscules (capitales) – 7 largeurs de bec*
- *angle de la plume – 45°*
- *lettre **o** de forme – inclinée ovale*
- *inclinaison – 5° à peu près*
- *empattements – traits simples d'entrée et de sortie*

LETRA ITÁLICA

- *altura de la x 5 anchos por altura, ascendentes 8 anchos por altura, descendentes 8 anchos por altura*
- *altura de las mayúsculas – 7 anchos por altura*
- *ángulo de la pluma – 45°*
- *inclinada – 5° aproximadamente*
- *la forma de la letra **o** – un óvalo inclinado*
- *gracias – trazos sencillos de comienzo y terminación*

- *x-height – 3·5 nib widths, ascenders 5·5 nib widths, descenders 5·5 nib widths*
- *nib angle – 30°*
- *slant – upright*
- *letter **o** form – round*
- *serifs – simple entry and exit strokes*

ONCIALES

- *hauteur d'x de 3·5 largeurs de bec, ascendantes de 5·5 largeurs de bec, descendantes de 5·5 largeurs de bec*
- *angle de la plume – 30°*
- *lettre **o** de forme – ronde*
- *inclinaison – droite*
- *empattements – traits simples d'entrée et de sortie*

UNCIALES

- *altura de la x 3·5 anchos por altura, ascendentes 5·5 anchos por altura, descendentes 5·5 anchos por altura*
- *ángulo de la pluma – 30°*
- *la forma de la letra **o** – redonda*
- *inclinada – recta*
- *gracias – trazos sencillos de comienzo y terminación*

Common errors to avoid

Foundational or Round Hand

Arch starts too far down on the downstroke.

Exit strokes too curvy.

Letter too narrow and third stroke too curvy.

First stroke too straight, bowl too large.

Gothic Black Letter

Third stroke too far down, making bowl too large.

Arch too curved; it should be straighter.

Letter starts too high, resulting in ugly crossbar. Base stroke too curvy.

Tail too large, the curve should be more compressed.

Foundational ou Ronde

Arceau commençant trop bas sur le trait descendant.

Traits de sortie trop incurvés.

Lettre trop étroite et troisième trait trop incurvé.

Premier trait trop droit, panse trop grande.

Lettres noires gothiques

Troisième trait trop bas, rendant la panse trop grande.

Arceau trop incurvé; il devrait être plus droit.

La lettre commence trop haut, ce qui enlaidit la traverse, et trait de base trop incurvé.

Queue trop grande, la courbe devrait être plus comprimée.

Fundacional o redonda

Arco empieza demasiado abajo en el trazo vertical.

Trazo terminal demasiado curvo.

Letra demasiado estrecha y tercer trazo demasiado curvo.

Primer trazo demasiado recto, espacio interno demasiado grande.

Letra negra gótica

Tercer trazo demasiado abajo, hace el espacio interno demasiado grande.

Arco demasiado curvo; debería ser más recto.

La letra empieza demasiada alta lo que resulta en una tilde fea. Trazo base es demasiado curvo

Cola demasiado larga, la curva debe ser más comprimida.

Italic

r f x z

Arch wrong shape, stroke should start from the baseline and push up.

Top and tail too curved, making fish-hooks. Cross-bar starts too high.

Strokes too curvy. Only entry and exit strokes should curve.

Diagonal stroke too narrow (nib not turned to 10°).

Italiques

Arceau de forme incorrecte, le trait doit commencer à partir de la ligne de pied et remonter.

Queues trop incurvées, formant des hameçons. La traverse commence trop haut.

Traits trop incurvés. Seuls les traits d'entrée et de sortie doivent être incurvés.

Trait diagonal trop étroit (la plume n'est pas pivotée à 10°).

Italica

Forma del arco incorrecta, el trazo debe empezar en la línea base y ascender.

Parte de arriba y cola demasiado curvas, forman anzuelos. La tilde empieza demasiado alto.

Trazos demasiado curvos. Solamente los trazos de comienzo y terminación deben ser curvos.

Trazo diagonal demasiado estrecho (no se ha girado la pluma a 10°).

Uncial

ı s ð k

Entry and exit strokes too curvy.

All strokes too curved, making an enclosed letter.

Second stroke too far right; the letter looks as if it is falling.

Bowl too large, making an unbalanced letter.

Onciales

Traits d'entrée et de sortie trop incurvés.

Tous les traits sont trop incurvés, formant une lettre close.

Deuxième trait trop à droite, on dirait que la lettre va tomber.

Panse trop grande, ce qui déséquilibre la lettre.

Uncial

Trazos de comienzo y terminación demasiado curvos.

Todos los trazos demasiado curvos, forman una letra encapsulada.

Segundo trazo demasiado a la derecha; Parece como si la letra se estuviera cayendo.

Espacio interno demasiado grande, forma una letra desequilibrada.

31

Good Luck   Happy New Year

Robert Sophie Thomas Ursula

Andrea Bertie Christy Daniel Emma

Bonne Année meilleurs voeux

felicitaciones los mejores deseos

Place a piece of layout paper over these guidelines to practise your letters – it will save you drawing your own lines. These lines are for a Manuscript nib size 1½.

30° x h q p

Placez une feuille de papier translucide sur ces lignes directrices pour vous entraîner à former vos lettres, ce qui vous évite d'avoir à tracer vos propres lignes. Ces lignes sont prévues pour la plume Manuscrit de taille 1½.

Coloque una hoja de papel de calco sobre estas líneas de guía para practicar las letras, le ahorrará tener que dibujar sus propias líneas de guía. Estas líneas son para un plumín para Manuscritos de 1½.

Place a piece of layout paper over these guidelines to practise your letters – it will save you drawing your own lines. These lines are for Manuscript nib size 1½.

45°

o h p p

Placez une feuille de papier translucide sur ces lignes directrices pour vous entraîner à former vos lettres, ce qui vous évite d'avoir à tracer vos propres lignes. Ces lignes sont prévues pour la plume Manuscrit de taille 1½.

Coloque una hoja de papel de calco sobre estas líneas de guía para practicar las letras, le ahorrará tener que dibujar sus propias líneas de guía. Estas líneas son para un plumín para Manuscritos de 1½.

Place a piece of layout paper over these guidelines to practise your letters – it will save you drawing your own lines. These lines are for a Manuscript nib size 1½.

x h p p

45°

Placez une feuille de papier translucide sur ces lignes directrices pour vous entraîner à former vos lettres, ce qui vous évite d'avoir à tracer vos propres lignes. Ces lignes sont prévues pour la plume Manuscrit de taille 1½.

Coloque una hoja de papel de calco sobre estas líneas de guía para practicar las letras, le ahorrará tener que dibujar sus propias líneas de guía. Estas líneas son para un plumín para Manuscritos de 1½.

Guidelines for Uncial   Lignes directrice   Líneas de guía

Place a piece of layout paper over these guidelines to practise your letters – it will save you drawing your own lines. These lines are for a Manuscript nib size 1½.

o b p

30°

Placez une feuille de papier translucide sur ces lignes directrices pour vous entraîner à former vos lettres, ce qui vous évite d'avoir à tracer vos propres lignes. Ces lignes sont prévues pour la plume Manuscrit de taille 1½.

Coloque una hoja de papel de calco sobre estas líneas de guía para practicar las letras, le ahorrará tener que dibujar sus propias líneas de guía. Estas líneas son para un plumín para Manuscritos de 1½.